2nd EDITION
INCREDIBLE ENGLISH S
Starter Class Book

1	Hello!	2
2	My pencil case	12
3	Funny faces!	22
4	Hello, robot!	32
5	Pets	42
6	Apples and oranges	52
	Songs	62
	Language Summary	63

Eng/196

Sarah Phillips

OXFORD
UNIVERSITY PRESS

Lesson 2

1 Stick. Listen and play Bingo. 1.4

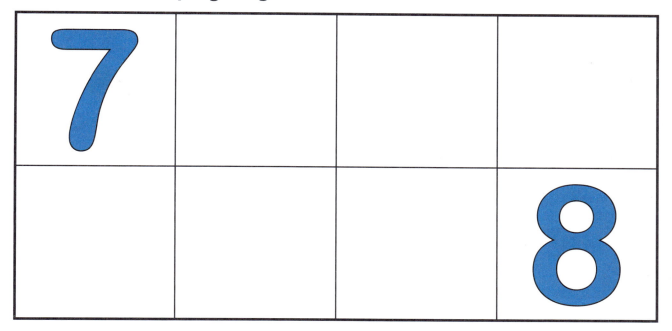

2 Draw. Listen and number. 1.5

Lesson 3

1 Listen and point. 🔘 1.6 **2** Act.

Hello, Kitty!

4 Unit 1

Lesson 4

1 Find and say. Listen and check. 🔊 1.7

2 Listen and number. 🔊 1.8
3 Listen and repeat. 🔊 1.9

Hello, Bing! Goodbye, Bing!

Unit 1

Lesson 5

1 Listen and point. 1.10 Listen again and repeat.

2 Listen and follow the route. 1.11

6 Unit 1

Where's Titch? Here!

Lesson 6

1 Match. Listen and check. 🔊 1.12 Listen again and repeat.

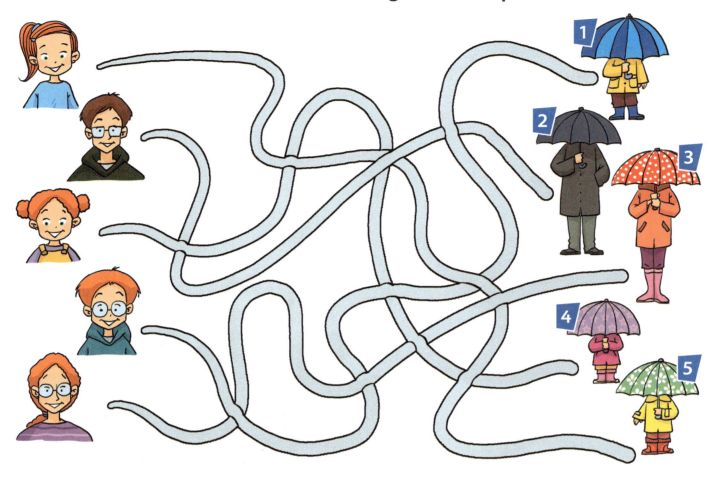

2 Draw your family. Say.

Unit 1 | 7

Lesson 7

Autumn Colours

1 Listen and point. 1.13
2 Listen and answer. 1.14

1
2
3
4
5

8 Unit 1

red   orange   yellow   brown   green

Learning through English: Science

Lesson 8

1 Make a leaf collage.

Unit 1 9

Lesson 9

1 Listen and point.  1.15
2 Listen again and sing.

Following instructions

Lesson 10

1 Who is it? Listen and check. 1.16

2 Listen and point. 1.17 Say.

3 Listen and colour. 1.18 Say.

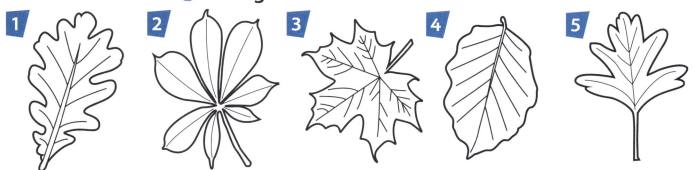

Revision – Unit 1 | 11

2 My pencil case

Lesson 1

1 Listen and find. 🔊 1.19 Listen, point and repeat. 🔊 1.20
2 Listen and chant. 🔊 1.21

pencil rubber crayon ruler notebook pencil case

Lesson 2

1 Stick. Listen and play Bingo. 🎧 1.22

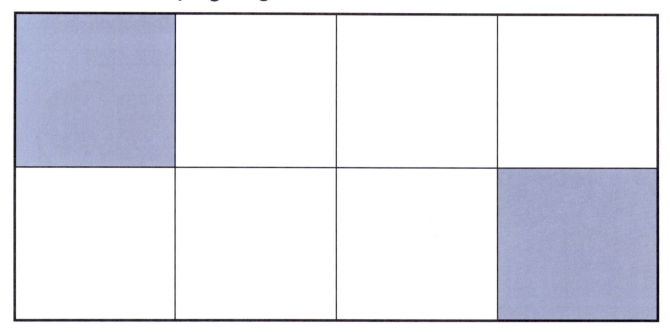

2 Listen, find and colour. 🎧 1.23

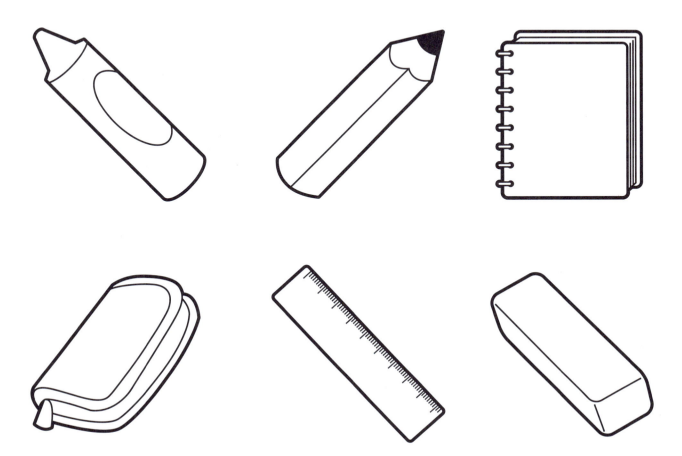

Unit 2 · 13

Lesson 3

1 Listen and point. 🔊 1.24   **2** Act.

The mouse

Lesson 4

1 Find and say. Listen and check. 🔊 1.25

2 Listen and circle. 🔊 1.26

3 Listen and repeat. 🔊 1.27

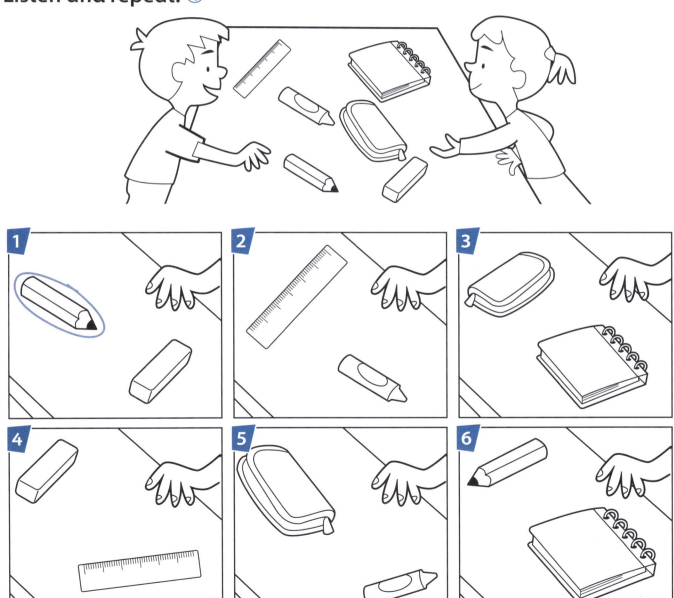

Pass the pencil, please. Here! Thanks!

Unit 2 | 15

Lesson 5

1 Listen and point. 🔊 1.28 **Listen again and repeat.**

2 Listen and say who. 🔊 1.29 **Listen again and repeat.**

16 Unit 2

I've got a crayon!

1 Draw.

2 Listen and match. 🔊 1.30 Listen again and repeat.

3 Draw your pencil case. Say.

Unit 2 17

Lesson 7

Colour mixing

1 Listen and point. 1.31
2 Listen, find and answer. 1.32

18 Unit 2

blue purple black white grey pink

Lesson 8

1 Make a rainbow.

Learning through English: Art

Unit 2 19

Lesson 9

1 Listen and point. 1.33
2 Listen again and sing.

20 Unit 2

Tidying up

1 Listen and follow the route. 1.34

2 Listen and circle. 1.35 Say.

3 Listen and colour. 1.36 Say.

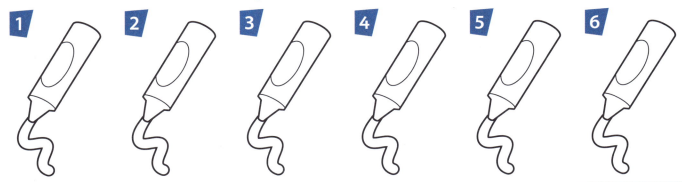

Lesson 1

3 Funny faces!

1 Listen and find. 🔊 1.37   Listen, point and repeat. 🔊 1.38
2 Listen and chant. 🔊 1.39

22

face   eyes   ears   nose   mouth   hair

1 Stick. Listen and play Bingo. 🔊 1.40

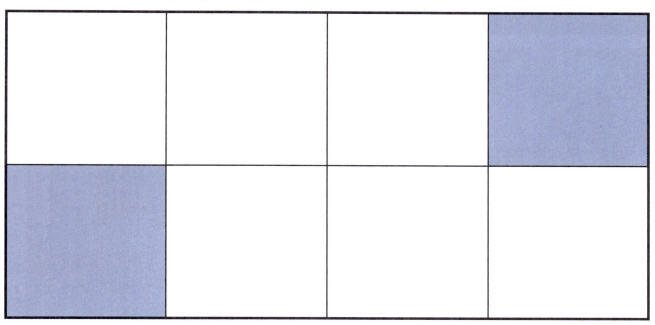

2 Listen and colour. 🔊 1.41

Lesson 3

1 Listen and point. 1.42 **2** Act.

Titch is Kitty!

Lesson 4

1 Find and say. Listen and check. 🔊 1.43

2 Listen and circle. 🔊 1.44

Close your eyes. Open your mouth. Look!

Unit 3

Lesson 5

1 Listen and say who. 🔊 1.45

2 Listen, point and repeat. 🔊 1.46

3 Listen and find. Say the number. 🔊 1.47

Unit 3

He's got a black face. She's got pink ears.

Lesson 6

1 Listen and colour the key. 1.48 Colour the pictures.

2 Paint your face. Say.

Unit 3

Lesson 7

Drawing a face

1 Listen and point. 🔊 1.49

2 Listen and say the number. 🔊 1.50

1
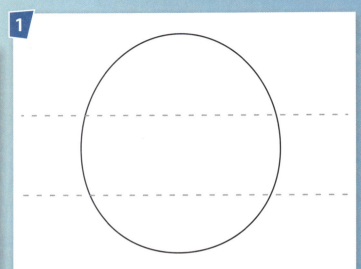

2

3

4

5

28 | Unit 3

big eyes, small mouth, happy, sad

3 Listen and find. 🔊 1.51

1

2

3

4

Learning through English: Art

Lesson 8

1 Make a mix-and-match book.

Unit 3 | 29

Lesson 9

1 Listen and point. 1.52
2 Listen again and sing.

Personal hygiene

Lesson 10

1 Listen and number. 1.53

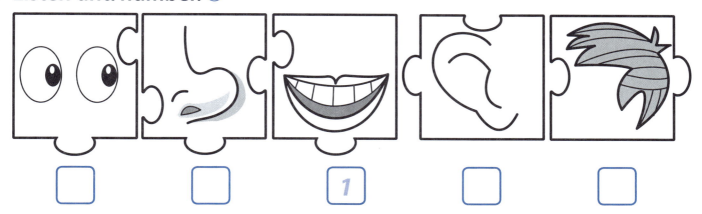

☐   ☐   *1*   ☐   ☐

2 Listen and colour. 1.54 Say.

1   2

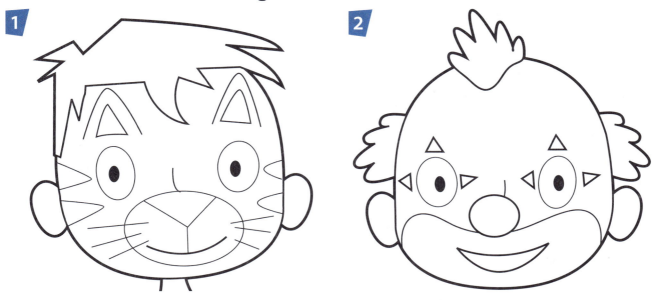

3 Find the differences in picture 2.

Revision – Unit 3   31

4 Hello, robot!

Lesson 1

1 **Listen and find.** 🔊 2.1 **Listen, point and repeat.** 🔊 2.2
2 **Listen and chant.** 🔊 2.3

walk   run   jump   dance   sing   climb   play football   say hello

32

1	2	3	4
5	6		

Lesson 2

1 Stick. Listen and play Bingo. 2.4

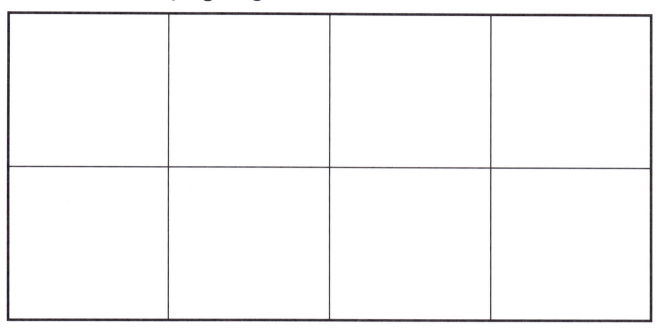

2 Listen and draw a line. 2.5

Unit 4

Lesson 3

1 Listen and point. 2.6 **2** Act.

Kitty and the robot

34 Unit 4

Lesson 4

1 Find and say. Listen and check. 🎧 2.7

2 Match. Listen and check. 🎧 2.8

3 Listen and repeat. 🎧 2.9

It's my turn. It's your turn.

Unit 4 | 35

Lesson 5

1 **Listen and point.** 2.10 **Listen again and repeat.**

2 **Listen and answer.** 2.11

3 **Listen and repeat.** 2.12

36 Unit 4

It can play football. It can't sing.

Lesson 6

1 Listen and tick ✓ or cross ✗. 2.13

2 Draw a robot. Say.

Unit 4 37

Lesson 7

Money

1 Listen and find. 🔊 2.14

 = £1

 = £2

 = £3

 = £4

= £5

 = £6

 = £7

 = £8

ball   car   teddy   £ (pound)

2 Listen and write the number. 2.15

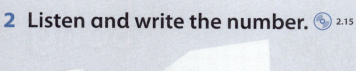

1 Make and play.

Learning through English: Maths

Lesson 8

Unit 4 39

Lesson 9

1 Listen and point. 🎧 2.16
2 Listen again and sing.

40 Unit 4

Showing your feelings

Lesson 10

1 Listen and number. 🔊 2.17 Say.

2 Listen and tick ✓ or cross ✗. 🔊 2.18 Say.

3 Listen, find and complete. 🔊 2.19

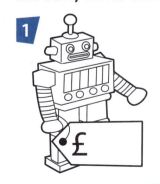   

Revision – Unit 4

Lesson 2

1 Stick. Listen and play Bingo. 2.23

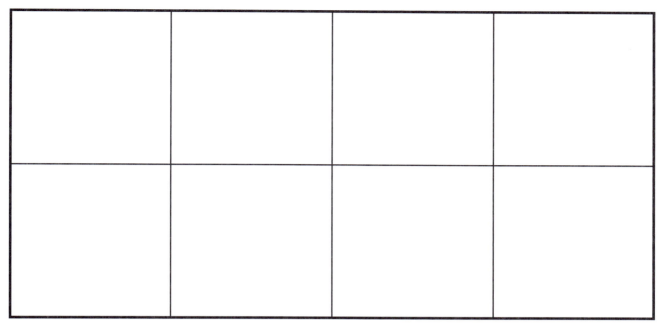

2 What's next? Draw and say.

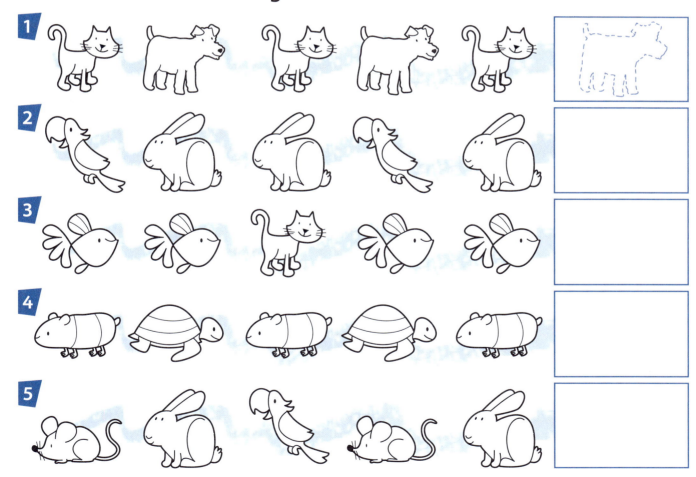

Unit 5 — 43

Lesson 3

1 **Listen and point.** 2.24 2 **Act.**

What a noise!

Lesson 4

1 Find and say. Listen and check. 2.25

2 Listen and circle. 2.26 Say.

Can I have a parrot? Yes, OK. No, sorry.

Unit 5

Lesson 5

1 Listen and point. 🎧 2.27 Listen again and repeat.

2 Listen and number. 🎧 2.28 Say.

46 Unit 5

What's your favourite animal?   A rabbit.

Lesson 6

1 Match. Listen and check. 2.29 Say.

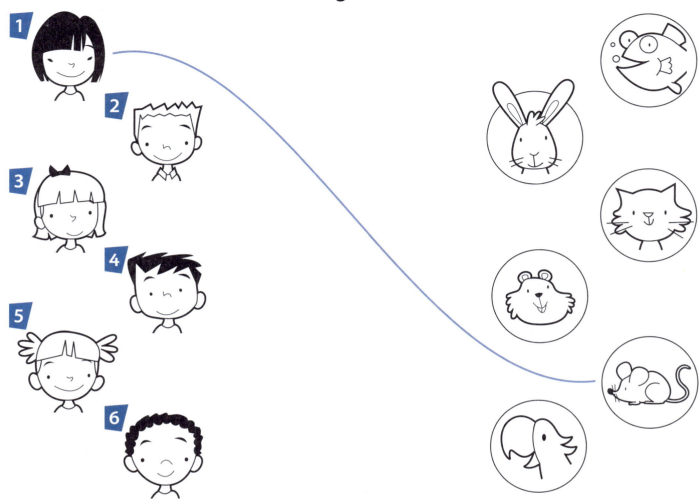

2 Draw your favourite animal. Say.

Unit 5 | 47

Lesson 7
Feathers

1 Listen and find. 🔊 2.30
2 Match. Then listen and say *Yes* or *No*. 🔊 2.31

48 Unit 5

feather   penguin   duck   peacock

Lesson 8

1 Make a bird collage.

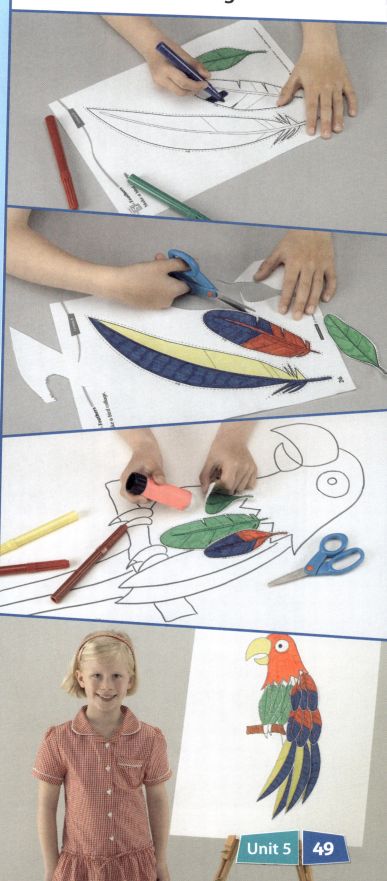

Learning through English: Science

Unit 5 49

Lesson 9

1 Listen and point. 2.32
2 Listen again and sing.

50 Unit 5 Caring for your pet

Lesson 10

1 Match. Say.

2 Listen and number. Say. 2.33

3 Listen and colour. 2.34

Revision – Unit 5   51

Apples and oranges

Lesson 1

1 **Listen and find.** 🔊 2.35 **Listen, point and repeat.** 🔊 2.36
2 **Listen and chant.** 🔊 2.37

apples   bananas   oranges   lemons   tomatoes   peppers   carrots   peas

Lesson 2

1 Stick. Listen and play Bingo. 2.38

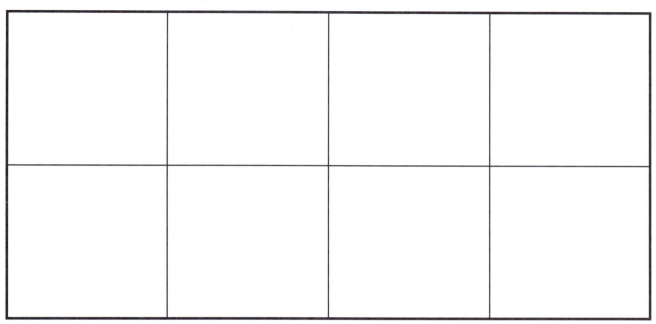

2 Count and write. Then listen and answer Yes or No. 2.39

3 Listen and colour. 2.40

Unit 6 53

Lesson 3

1 Listen and point. 2.41 **2** Act.

The milkshake

Lesson 4

1 Find and say. Listen and check. 🔊 2.42

2 Listen and draw 🍎 or 🥛. 🔊 2.43 Listen again and repeat.

I'm hungry! I'm thirsty!

Unit 6 | 55

Lesson 5

1 Listen and point. 2.44

2 Listen and repeat. 2.45

2 Listen and follow. Say the name. 2.46

56 Unit 6

I like peas. I don't like carrots.

Lesson 6

1 Listen and draw ⌣ or ⌢. 🔊 2.47 Say.

2 Draw food you like and you don't like. Say.

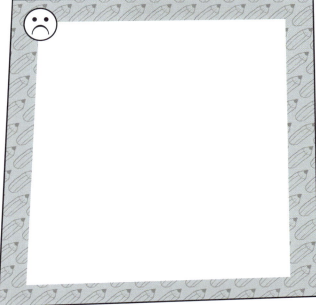

Unit 6 57

Lesson 7

Carroll diagrams

1 Listen and point. 2.48

Lesson 8

1 Make a Carroll diagram.

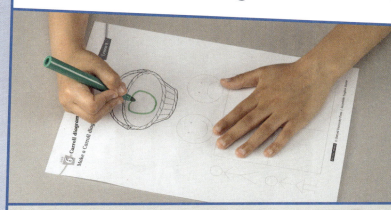

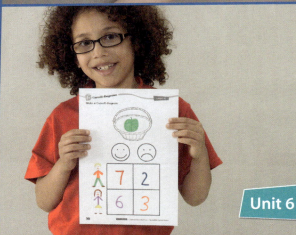

2 Listen and answer. 2.49

Learning through English: Maths

Unit 6 | 59

Lesson 9

1. Listen and point. 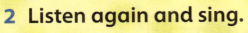 2.50
2. Listen again and sing.

Eating a varied diet

Lesson 10

1 Listen and circle. 2.51

   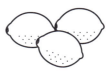

2 Listen and match. 2.52

2 Listen and complete. 2.53

Revision – Unit 6

Songs

Page 10 – 1.15

Stand up and point!
Point, point!
Stand up and point!
Shh, shh, good.

Sit down and listen!
Listen, listen!
Sit down and listen!
Shh, shh, good.

Stand up, come here!
Come here, come here!
Stand up, come here!
Shh, shh, good.

Sit down, be quiet!
Be quiet, be quiet!
Sit down, be quiet!
Shh, shh, good.

Page 20 – 1.33

Time to tidy up,
Time to tidy up,
Everybody stop!
Everybody help!

Put your pencils in the box,
Put your notebooks on the shelf,
Everybody stop!
Everybody help!

Put your crayons in the box,
Put your books on the shelf,
Everybody stop!
Everybody help!

Page 30 – 1.52

Clean your teeth in the morning,
Clean your teeth in the morning,
Clean your teeth in the morning,
Clean your teeth like this!

Wash your face in the morning,
Wash your face in the morning,
Wash your face in the morning,
Wash your face like this!

Brush your hair in the morning,
Brush your hair in the morning,
Brush your hair in the morning,
Brush your hair like this!

Wash your hands in the morning,
Wash your hands in the morning,
Wash your hands in the morning,
Wash your hands like this!

Page 40 – 2.16

Dance with me, I'm happy,
I'm happy,
I'm happy.
Dance with me, I'm happy,
I'm happy, dance with me.

Walk with me, I'm sad,
I'm sad,
I'm sad.
Walk with me, I'm sad,
I'm sad, walk with me.

Sit with me, I'm tired,
I'm tired,
I'm tired.
Sit with me, I'm tired,
I'm tired, sit with me.

Run with me, I'm scared,
I'm scared,
I'm scared.
Run with me, I'm scared,
I'm scared, run with me.

Page 50 – 2.32

I love my cat like this,
I love my cat,
I love my cat,
I love my cat like this!

I love my turtle like this,
I love my turtle,
I love my turtle,
I love my turtle like this!

I love my rabbit like this,
I love my rabbit,
I love my rabbit,
I love my rabbit like this!

I love my dog like this,
I love my dog,
I love my dog,
I love my dog like this!

Page 60 – 2.50

Two, four, six, eight,
Put something green on your plate.
Peas are green, peppers are too,
Peas and peppers are good for you!

Two, four, six, eight,
Put something yellow on your plate.
Lemons are yellow, bananas are too,
Lemons and bananas are good for you!

Two, four, six, eight,
Put something red on your plate.
Tomatoes are red, apples are too,
Tomatoes and apples are good for you!

Two, four, six, eight,
Put something orange on your plate.
Carrots are orange, oranges are too,
Carrots and oranges are good for you!

Language Summary

		Vocabulary	Structures
1	**Hello!**	**Characters:** Mum, Dad, Fred, Flo, Titch, Kitty **Numbers:** 1, 2, 3, 4, 5, 6, 7, 8 **CLIL (Science):** red, brown, orange, yellow, green	**Where's Titch?** **Here!** Hello, Bing! Goodbye, Bing!
2	**My pencil case**	**Classroom:** pencil, rubber, crayon, ruler, notebook, pencil case **CLIL (Art):** blue, pink, purple, black, white, grey	**I've got a crayon!** Pass the pencil, please. Here! Thanks!
3	**Funny faces!**	**Face:** face, eyes, ears, nose, mouth, hair **CLIL (Art):** big eyes, small mouth, happy, sad	**He's got a black face.** **She's got pink ears.** Close your eyes. Open your mouth. Look!
4	**Hello, robot!**	**Abilities:** run, jump, dance, play football, climb, say hello, walk, sing **CLIL (Maths):** teddy, car, ball, £ (pound)	**It can play football.** **It can't sing.** It's my turn. It's your turn.
5	**Pets**	**Animals:** turtle, fish, cat, dog, mouse, parrot, rabbit, hamster **CLIL (Science):** feather, penguin, duck, peacock	**What's your favourite animal? A rabbit.** Can I have a parrot? Yes, OK. No, sorry.
6	**Apples and oranges**	**Food:** apples, bananas, oranges, lemons, tomatoes, peppers, carrots, peas	**I like peas.** **I don't like carrots.** I'm hungry! I'm thirsty!

Great Clarendon Street, Oxford, OX2 6DP, United Kingdom

Oxford University Press is a department of the University of Oxford.
It furthers the University's objective of excellence in research, scholarship,
and education by publishing worldwide. Oxford is a registered trade
mark of Oxford University Press in the UK and in certain other countries

© Oxford University Press 2011

The moral rights of the author have been asserted

First published in 2011

2015 2014 2013 2012 2011
10 9 8 7 6 5 4 3 2 1

No unauthorized photocopying

All rights reserved. No part of this publication may be reproduced, stored
in a retrieval system, or transmitted, in any form or by any means, without
the prior permission in writing of Oxford University Press, or as expressly
permitted by law, by licence or under terms agreed with the appropriate
reprographics rights organization. Enquiries concerning reproduction outside
the scope of the above should be sent to the ELT Rights Department, Oxford
University Press, at the address above

You must not circulate this work in any other form and you must impose
this same condition on any acquirer

Links to third party websites are provided by Oxford in good faith and for
information only. Oxford disclaims any responsibility for the materials
contained in any third party website referenced in this work

ISBN: 978 0 19 4442053

Printed in China

This book is printed on paper from certified and well-managed sources

ACKNOWLEDGEMENTS

Main illustrations by: Gustavo Mazali pp.2, 3, 4, 5, 6, 7, 11 (top), 12, 14, 15 (top), 16, 17, 21, 22, 24, 25 (top), 26 (top), 31 (bottom), 32, 34, 35, 36 (top), 42, 44, 45 (top), 46 (top), 52, 54, 55 (top), 56, 61.

Other illustrations by: Kathy Baxendale p.29, 46 (bottom); John Haslam pp.11 (leaves), 13, 15 (bottom), 23, 25 (bottom), 26 (bottom), 27, 28, 31 (top), 33, 36 (bottom), 37, 41, 43, 45 (bottom), 47, 51, 53, 55 (bottom), 57; Heather Heyworth/The Bright Agency pp.10, 20, 30, 40, 50, 60.

Commissioned photos by: MM Studio pp.9, 18, 19, 38, 39, 49, 58, 59.

The Publishers would also like to thank the following for their kind permission to reproduce photographs and other copyright material: Alamy pp.8-9 (yellow beech leaf/WILDLIFE GmbH, brown oak leaf/Arco Images GmbH), 48 (black penguin feather/yellow parrot feather/Arco Images GmbH, blue peacock feather/Juniors Bildarchiv, white feather/Ian Skelton), 49 (parrot in flight/parrot feathers inset/Marco Simoni/Robert Harding Picture Library Ltd, peacock/F. Wagner/F1online digitale Bildagentur GmbH); Getty Images pp.49 (duck feather inset/Nacivet/Photographer's Choice); Naturepl.com p.49 (peacock feather inset/Ashok Jain, penguin and penguin feather inset/Fred Olivier); Oxford University Press pp.8-9 (maple leaf, chestnut leaf), 28, 48 (red feather, green duck feather, peacock eye feather, brown duck feather); Photolibrary pp.49 (duck/Stephane Hubert/Digital Light Source).

Cover illustration by: Gustavo Mazali